No Lovelier Melody Ever Was Known

A Month of 96 Poems in Amphibrachic Tetrameter Catalectic

No Lovelier Melody Ever Was Known

A Month of 96 Poems in Amphibrachic Tetrameter Catalectic

(9/23/22–10/24/22)

MARTIN BIDNEY

Dialogic
Poetry
Press

Copyright © 2023 by Martin Bidney
Dialogic Poetry Press
Vestal, New York

All Rights Reserved

ISBN 13: 979-8376513354

Printed in the United States of America

Available from Amazon at
http://www.amazon.com/dp/

Contents

Introduction	**9**
1 What's the rhythm used in this book?	**9**
2 Focuses of Interest	**11**
2.1 Joy	*11*
2.2 Reimagining Scripture:	
Judaeo-Christo-Islamic Tradition	*13*
2.3 The Boundless and the Beating Heart	*13*
2.4 Verse Journaling	*14*
Scripture	**16**
1 Ancient Roamin' Pomes	**20**
2 A1C	**21**
3 Grecian-earned	**22**
4 Rosh Ha-Shanah	**23**
5 Improvisation	**24**
6 Accounting	**25**
7 Acknowledgment	**26**
8 Commentary	**27**
9 Beautiful	**28**
10 Breathing	**29**

11 Chatinyan 1	30
12 Psalm	31
13 Better	32
14 Ornamental	33
15 Remorphing	34
16 Essential	35
17 Solomon	36
18 Receive	37
19 Hands 1	38
20 Songs	39
21 Rivers	40
23 Strange	42
24 Line	43
25 Steepled	45
26 Untitled	46
27 Touched	48
28 Otis	49
29 Workplace 1	50
30 Workplace 2	51
31 Kafka 1	52
32 Kafka 2	53
33 House	54
34 Bush 1	55
35 Kafka 3	56
36 Kafka 4	57
37 Kafka 5	58
38 Kafka 6	59
39 Hands 2	60
40 Computer	61
41 Tactics	62
42 Kafka 7	63
43 Sudden	64

44 Prayer	65
45 Preparation	66
46 Notes	67
47 Bibliomancer 1	68
48 Bibliomancer 2	69
49 Bibliomancer 3	70
50 Biography	72
51 Cat	73
52 St(art)	74
53 Awaking	75
54 Thracian	76
55 Presentiments	77
56 Give	78
57 Timeful	79
58 Ranakpur	80
59 Windows	81
60 Tech	82
61 Experiment	83
62 Schoolmaster	84
63 Benefits	85
64 Instructional	86
65 Cholent	87
66 Shadows	88
67 Scripture	89
68 Message	90
69 Marigolds	91
70 Refrain	92
71 Chatinyan 2	93
72 Recompense	94
73 Pumpkin	95
74 Diversity	96
75 Sphere	97

76 Squirrel 1	98
77 Similitudes	99
78 Journey	100
79 Squirrel 2	101
80 Solace	102
81 Newspaper 1	104
82 Newspaper 2	105
83 Better	106
84 Guarded	107
85 Hollowed	108
86 Played	109
87 Barrett	110
88 Proverb	111
89 Ruminations	112
90 "Otumnal"	113
91 Sappho	114
92 Half-awake	115
93 Prima	116
94 Bush 2	117
95 Bush 3	118
96 Proverbs	119

Introduction

1 What's the rhythm used in this book?

In my 79 years of life so far I've probably never had a more productive period of writing (with the single exception of the 13 days it took me to write the 108 *Wordsongs of Jewish Thought*) than while creating this collection. It's a book of ec-stasy, a Greek-derived word (*ek-stasis*) that means you're "beside yourself" with joy.

Why the exhilarated mood and presto tempo? The answer is in the verse form I use in 96 poems. An explorer of rare verse forms, I love coming up with "endangered species" of stanza construction, gorgeous rhythmic-life creations in danger of going extinct. During the past month I've been in love with a meter called the amphibrachic tetrameter catalectic, for a joyful autumn month in upstate New York.

You can hear the spirit in my book title: "A Lovelier Melody Never Was Heard." So let me explain right away what rhythm is featured here.

First word: amphibrachic. This means "made out of amphibrachs." And what's an amphibrach? It goes like this:

la-LA-la. "A Lovelier Melody Never Was Heard" has this rhythm: "la-LA-la, la-LA-la, la-LA-la, la-LA."

Honestly, that's all there is to it. No rocket science (to coin a phrase). Why does the thing have a complicated-sounding Greek-derived name? Because it was the ancient Greeks who got us started thinking about recurrent rhythms (meters) in a systematic way. The rhythm itself, like many genius-level inventions, seems quite simple and normal once it has been thought of. "la-LA-la, la-LA-la, la-LA-la, la-LA." Comic strip tiger Hobbes could explain it to six-year-old Calvin with no difficulty, simply by saying it.

Let's continue with the label. "Tetrameter" = meter or rhythm with four beats. A beat is what I've capitalized in each foot, a syllable that is felt to be STRONG or HEAVY. When you say, "hel-LO!" you've begun with a weak syllable and ended with a STRONG one. If you say, "MA-ry," you've begun with a STRONG syllable and ended with a weak one. If you add, "how-ARE-you?" it's an amphibrach you've made: "la-LA-la," or "weak-STRONG-weak."

One more word to go and we're done with our lesson in Greek. Notice that "A Lovelier Melody Never Was Heard" doesn't end with a complete amphibrach, It ends not with "la-LA-la" but simply with "la-LA." So the last foot in our verse line has not three syllables but two. There's a syllable missing. And the Greek word for "missing syllable" is "catalexis." Any verse line that ends with a foot having a missing syllable is called "catalectic."

Voilà! We now know what's meant by an "amphibrachic tetrameter catalectic," and you're ready to hear my poems in this book. Actually, if you have some experience with musical beats in wordsongs, you heard the rhythm already in my Calvin-and-Hobbes demonstration by saying it aloud. Every poem in this book must be heard because they're all wordsongs. Best to say a poem out loud, or hear an inner voice that acts it out. It's quite a foot-tapping rhythm. I'm a folk fiddler and it makes me think of square dances. I wrote daily poems in this beat for a month without ever getting bored: the rhythm always makes me want to start typing word-music. Hey, it's happening right now—listen:

Explaining to readers a rhythmical beat
Returned me to days entertaining and sweet.
Dear Muse of the Barn-Dance, I'm grateful to you,
Fair Lady I gladly and ardently greet.

After our lesson in Greek, it felt right to thank one of the ancient mythic Muses, patrons of the arts and culture.

2 Focuses of Interest

2.1 Joy

I began with a remark on the Greek word "ecstasy," indicating a feeling of being "beside yourself" with joy. That's because all the things I do in my month of amphibrachic experimentation are subsets of the joy produced by the jaunty meter. Poem lengths vary, topics vary, and rhyme patterns vary. Poem 61, for example, tells of the unusual introduction of the rhyme pattern typical of works by the sometimes wistful and melancholic Persian poet Omar (cf. my *Owed to Omar*). But the general cheerfulness of my temperament tends to persist. Even a jeremiad on trendy stylistic flaws (poem 62) is jocular, and poem 63, on the benefits of aging, is less ironic than welcoming. When a memory brings joy, as in my reply to a mandolin-playing facebook friend with whom I've played fiddle for decades (poem 87), the jokes just pour out.

Poems 1, 2, and 3, warm-up exercises, are light in tone: a reply to a facebook friend, a "strategy" to get lower daily sugar ratings (cf. poem 27), and a playful metaphor of my mentality in writing. Poem 5 conveys a casual, relaxed approach to receiving and welcoming whatever comes to me when I compose. An easygoing, pragmatic approach to daily life appears in poem 6. Similarly, in poem 22 a lighthearted "parable" lets me play with a neo-scriptural approach to mundane events. In poem 23 I affirm the computer and keyboard as modern miracles worthy of poets Persian, Hebrew, or Greek (cf. poem 40).

In Poems 28–30 I prize the daily blessings of having a beloved pet and an attractive workplace; in 43 there's an epiphany of a rabbit, in 46 the vision of deer feeding and then running across my back yard. Poem 51 offers a whimsical "poetics of the cat" (cf. poems 81, 91) as poems 76 and 79 praise the squirrel. Poem 52 integrates getting up on a normal morning with a vision of an ideal mission. The map of my house that I sketch in poem 53 incorporates Kabbalistic and Sufi thinking about the "six directions" of our physical-and-spiritual world. Thoughts about washing windows get us into the theme of epiphanic "vision" in poem 59. Epiphanies of everyday life include a diabetic breakfast in poem 64.

Related to the pervasion of joy is the practice of play. In poem 57 wordplay arises from a curiosity about the ontology of time. Poem 88, "Proverb," plays around freely with the idea of wisdom sayings.

2.2 Reimagining Scripture: Judaeo-Christo-Islamic Tradition

Closely related to an attitude of affirmation is the approach my poems take to a renewal of scriptural traditions. Poem 56 tells of "the Psalm and the Gospel of Beauty." I like to think of poetry writing as the continuation of this tradition (see poem 7), and what has energized my imagining is the idea of a Judaeo-Christo-Islamic legacy of thoughts and ideas. All three religions take Abraham to be their father, and the Qur'an repeatedly depicts the Abrahamic scriptures as one in spirit. So poem 4, you'll see, is related to Judaism and poems 8, 9, 13, 16, 66, 70, 72, 74, 75, 77, 78, 80, 83, and 84 are linked to Islam, while poem 47 introduces Jesus via a Qur'anic citation, and poem 54 presents the Christian Emperor Leo. In poem 58 I bring in Jainism. Religion-related ethnic traditions, too, delight me, viz., poem 65 on "cholent," an item central to traditional Jewish cuisine.

Poem 12 brings together King David and the Qur'an. Hafeez, Plato, Euclid, and Genesis help me celebrate the sacredness of the "line" in poem 24, while in poem 26 I extend the implications of the "line" when commenting on a calligraphic painting by my friend and Sufi mentor, the renowned calligraphic artist Shahid Alam. In poem 44 on my prayerful willingness to wait for what comes, I join the Jewish and Islamic legacies of Sabbath and Surrender. Poem 45 offers a transition to the theme of breathing, which I'll develop in the next paragraph.

2.3 The Boundless and the Beating Heart

Though I don't teach the doctrines of any historical creed, I do extend the idea of scripture-writing in a way that accommodates my personal be-loving (rather than believing, unless these words are deemed essentially the same). My personal form of self- and world-awareness centers on what I call "the boundless and the beating heart," on breathing, the basis of meditation and the way we "take in" sky. Poems 9 and 10 give a sense of this.

Poem 11, which is about painting, introduces words like "prayer" and "worship" though the work may also be viewed as secular (cf. poems 71, 93). Similarly, poem 14 treats in a mode of awe the arrangement of decorative squashes I bought at a grocery, and poem 73 is a hymn to a pumpkin. In poem 15 I speak of the "remorphing of difeleth to lartife," which is a reshaping of life-death into art-life within the implied context of Orpheus (god of musical revival) and Morpheus (god of inspirational dreams), while Moses' sister the prophet Miriam and King Solomon's Biblical love song are plainly referenced. Poems 17 and 18 are tributes to this great love poet, such as I attempted also in *A Lover's Art*, where I newly translated Solomon's canticle.

Poem 19 lets me present my own aging hand as a natural work of art viewed as yet another theme for poetic scripture. Plato, Noah, Rumi, and other Sufis help me widen the scope of this art-religion in poem 20. Then in poem 25 my folded hands become an Abrahamic or nomadic tent (cf. poem 39). I view the Rivers of Eden in a context of poetic psychology (poem 21). In poems 47, 48, and 49 I express my debt to spiritual and poetic mentor-texts: the Qur'an, the Song of Solomon, and the Eclogues of Virgil.

2.4 Verse Journaling

In poems 31–38, 41–42, 50, 85, 92, and 96 I offer a set of experiments in trying to understand the appeal of an art that reveals a wholly mental world, a dream-performance of daily tensions and confrontation in a nighttime setting of oneiric logic. It's a well-known biographical datum that Kafka would laugh, at times, while writing and that he felt delivered, justified when and after performing his urgent solitary mission of presenting his world.

In poem 55 I look at a couple of odd psychosomatic symptoms of problems in earlier parts of my life; I do a bit of self-therapy, physical and mental, in my journal-poems. Like Kafka's collected works, mine too are an extended journal. Poem 60 is accordingly a transcript of an actual nightmare: monsters under the bed have yielded in the present century to demons in the computer. Poem 68, in contrast, is my versifying of an e-mail message from a friend, as poem 69 on marigolds replies to an e-mail from a gardener friend.

Verse journaling is in every way therapeutic, but it's more than that. You are creating meticulously crafted poems that are works of art. The art work so created may be that of the mental sufferer or the mental physician, it may be a clinical report or a proposed therapeutic regimen, what I call a "sermonette" addressed to oneself and anyone else who cares to listen. Physical and mental sufferer are the same person, and if they verse-journal together they are the co-creators of art.

A verse journal can bring back the happiest heart-moments you have ever known. Poem 82 celebrates the first cry of my newborn daughter Sarah. Poem 86 is another kind of epiphany, when I am suddenly flooded with happiness to think of how much pleasure I have shared, for 70 years, with my violin. Poem 89 commemorates, modestly, the recent meeting of a senior group for "Tea and Talk," a quiet and yet wonderful time that, if one were not a verse journaler, one might forget.

The verse journal accommodates the vagaries of daily change and the unpredictability of sudden mental translation. Thus poems 34, 94, and 95 are parts 1, 2, and 3 of a long-running meditation concerning the Biblical burning bush in which God was recognized by Moses. Fire is obviously worthy of interpretative comment, but the bush, in my view, requires possibly even deeper thought. Read the sequence and you'll see what I mean.

Poem 67, which I'll quote in a moment, ties together all the themes of this preface. It's called "Scripture" but could equally be titled "Verse Journal of a Boundless and a Beating Heart: The Performance of Joy." It's a statement by a wordsong maker who interprets "believing" as "beloving," an equation that brings forward the shared etymological derivation of the two words, with their single root of l-v.

Please remember to read all the poems aloud, so you hear the fiddle tunes! And maybe consider doing a verse journal of your own?

Scripture

Of themes preternatural, seekers inquire,
"When things viewed unclearly I feel the desire
More keenly to see and at last understand,
How best might I gratify such a demand?"

Well, whether a god's in existence or not

No Lovelier Melody 17

May well matter less for the health of your thought
Than seeking what's greater than "ego" or "me":
Your human imagining strive to set free!

I find it a comfort that scriptures exist.
And what are they good for? Whatever you've missed
By fearing for selfhood and fostering pride
You'll partly "fill in" with a possible guide.

Just open a wisdom book: I the Qur'an
Find rich in what fortune may offer: a dawn
May gleam, and a seed, inadvertently sown,
To flourish may soon have assurgently grown.

12/26/22

No Lovelier Melody Ever Was Known

1
Ancient Roamin' Pomes

trancelated by MB in reply to Jackson Tallmadge

Your fiddle is fretless—don't ever you fret.
Be tuneful, and soon you'll feel better, I bet.
Your kauphy will aid you by perking you up;
Just aim it correctly—quit missin' the cup!

9/23/22

2
A1C

I'm testing my sugar: it's—one sixty-five?
Oh, dreadful. Please help me: I need to survive!
Let's try it a second time: one thirty-three?
Well, that's a bit better. Be patient. We'll see

What next will appear—'tis one hundred nineteen!
My mood is more cheerful; I'm downright serene.
So don't be afraid of a voice crying, "Yikes!"
The tester who's patient will get what he likes …

9/25/22

3
Grecian-earned

Behold amphibrachic tetrameter cat-
alectic—a rabbit I pulled from the hat
Of magical rhythm to praise and to prize,
Enliven the ears and enlighten the eyes.

9/25/22

4
Rosh Ha-Shanah

with gratitude to Chabad Binghamton

Forgiveness for sin is the theme: New Year's Eve!
As pardon's a thing that my dreams don't believe,
I went to the service, the dinner, felt fine
Then rested. A blessing: the fruit of di- vine.

But wait—New Year's Day? I'm unwilling to rise.
It feels like reward from the Lord when one lies
Contènt with refreshment in life and in love—
I cannot quite hear a critique from above …

A knock at the door—and I ran, in surprise:
An Abraham-angel appeared to mine eyes:
We said the two blessings in Hebrew and he
One hundred bright calls of the trumpet for me

Brought forth with the skill that distinguishes art:
'Twas holy, the shofar—to soul 'twill impart
A pardon—a hint of the Garden, as well,
Where Abraham-angels continue to dwell.

9/26/22

5
Improvisation

Of "improvisation" the root, "unforeseen,"
Embodies a trust that whatever you mean,
With limited plot, to accomplish, will be
Imparted in art-making hearteningly.

Just looking ahead and foretelling the day
And feeling the songs that will come into play,
I'm tapping the beat and awaiting the thought
That pensive respect for the Muse will have brought.

It came, for what's dreamt by the grateful is great:
Poetical haven a happy estate
May lend when we view opportunity's port;
Our goal we attain when to Source we resort.

9/29/22

6
Accounting

With "thirty-eight purchases" total I've had
In amazon marketing, let us be glad
The twenty-ninth day of September displays
(In spite of a "zero" for several days)

Acknowledgment still that the month has achieved
What heart will encourage. The soul that believed
Examples the do-it-yourselfer provides
Got boosted morale from a tutor that guides.

Aut-hentic (that's "do it yourself" in the Greek),
The marketer sent by the Muse that you seek
Repeatedly proved that your average sales—
"One purchase per day"—shape an aim that avails.

9/29/22

7
Acknowledgment

Whoever distributes the meters to folk
Is kindred in spirit. A scrivener-stroke
Will wings overtower: ascensional height
Is planned for a power enclasped in delight.

When asked if our prayers are answered on high,
"Imaginer-Mage is a dancer," I cry,
"Who, shaking a spear as dear William had done,
A heaven attainer, will furnish the fun.

'Tis something I needed to sing, for within,
'I AM' means to be, to beget and begin.
Awaiting, creating, you 'angel' became:
Elated, instated, you're gaining a Name."

9/29/22

8
Commentary

Qur'an 25:47. And He it is Who maketh night a covering for you, and sleep repose, and maketh day a resurrection.

Of night He has fashioned protection for you,
And sleep for repose in perfection and, too,
The day as a blest resurrection will be
Of life that, reborn as the morn, you can see.

Awaking today I, delighted, surprised,
Felt more than had ever a body surmised:
A shock—there were suddenly "being" and "I"—
So startled my heart, one would need to ask why.

I woke from a Nothing—so heavy my sleep,
All dreams had been hid in oblivion deep.
The feel of a sheet on my hands—even more,
The sense of a thing not existent before!—

The strange revelation had passed from the mind;
Unlikely for me 'twould have been to re-find
The miracle-gift of the wonder I'd known
If not for the wisdom the scripture had shown.

9/29/22

9
Beautiful

*Qur'an 20:8. Allah! There is no God save Him.
His are the most beautiful names.*

Of Ultimate Being the ultimate name
May never in finite creation be known.
If all that we feel from the Ultimate came,
Of This we, at most, intimations are shown.

Of Ultimate Being the things that we sense
Themselves will remain the symbolical Names.
Their beauty immense, with a glory intense,
Their Source may evoke, as our poetry claims.

The Ultimate Name, the most beautiful kind,
We never can sing, I will say it again.
But all that, inspired, in creation we find
Reveals It obliquely to women and men.

What poets will feel to the Deep may come near,
What heartens the bard to the Highest comes nigh.
Uniquely, obliquely, you'll see It appear,
The Ultimate Love, in the heart and the sky.

9/30/22

10
Breathing

Assuming that gratitude adds to the joy
We get who our senses alertly employ,
Of nasal deep breathing I'll venture to chant
And, tranquil, divine what respiring may grant.

Both inward and outward the pleasure's more deep
The more we by counting true measure may keep.
Four seconds of each I prefer; and the beats,
When pleasingly numbered as eight, are my treats.

(I don't have a watch; are my estimates wrong?—
It doesn't much matter: proceed with your song.)
I crucially feel: for the plan to succeed,
Straight back and good posture you'll certainly need.

The rising and falling your lungs will refresh:
The blisses of body and mind intermesh.
A balm for your thought and a calm in the heart
Together engender the pleasure of art.

9/30/22

11
Chatinyan 1

In lava-like surge of a jewel display
The earth-love explodes in abundance today.
The colors of buds of the flowers and fruit
A storied Armenian glory will suit.

A showering dower will challenge the eyes:
A oneness of worship, of prayers and cries!
Of hillside and tree darker blue, black, and green
In forward-thrown shadow of scythe-man are seen.

The yellows and oranges lifting their light
Will threaten no desert; the pond-blue is bright.
The sides of the haystacks are curving: we say,
What smoothness and grace in our Nature's array!

Upheaval of world in vitality-thrill
The waterfall-gems had engendered to fill
The soul of the viewer, as only van Gogh
Before had been able, the A and the O.

9/30/22

12
Psalm

*Qur'an 17:55. [...] And We preferred some
of the Prophets above others, and unto David
We gave the Psalms.*

The rank uncontested of Prophet Preferred
Was given to one who, the strength of the word
In sweetness applying, the mountains made dance
And oceans made shout, and their being enhance.

The psalmer a loftier prophet became
When words he deployed in a way that a Name
Embodied of One who an infinite store
Of beautiful Names, the most glorious, wore.

His Names are the garments that only the heart
Can distantly view, yet they gleams can impart
Of that which our fallible eyes will confound,
And which to convey a most wonderful sound

Had David devised, that with instruments rare
Would bring to our singing a heavenly air:
Psalm hundred and fifty—the last—can a pure
Enjoyment arouse that will ever endure.

9/30/22

13
Better

Qur'an 27:89. Whoso bringeth a good deed will have better than its worth [....]

Warm singing's a merit but also a gift.
Our hymn's of the Lord. When with skill we express
The joy that with gratitude spirits will lift,
A child, as it were, has been born, whom we bless.

Be fruitful and multiply, poets, your fruit;
The Tree of our Lives you'll with power endue.
The cymbal and psaltery, timbrel and flute,
The barbiton, harp—they are comrades to you.

The branches that clash in the waves of a storm
Shall dance with the moon and the stars looking on;
What Morpheus dreamt will in Orpheus form
A herald of daybreak, the Cleaving of Dawn.

Your deed is a good one, but better 'twill be
When nature and spirit their energy blend
With what has been started, imparting a glee
That chants to the Youniverse, Welcome, my Friend!

9/30/22

14
Ornamental

No seventeenth-century Flemish display
Of tulips in dazzling eccentric array
More joy to the wonder-struck eye would convey
Than squashes and gourds I'm surveying today.

A five-section starfish, greens darker and light,
Is splashed with exuberant orange more bright
Than modern abstraction, expressionist, might
Include as a shock to enliven our sight.

A lumpier, squashier yellow-toned fest
Is striped with excrescences greening. We're blest
With one that, made lute-like, the striping
    compressed
With golden and green in competitive test.

An oval one's muted in hue. Lightest green
Long lines are dividers, let slicing be seen
Where yellow-white-verdant is brindling between
Apportionings, varied, of color serene.

A tinier, perfectly spherical gourd,
Dark-green every slicing-line, holds a reward:
Stained glass are the apertures, voicing accord,
With pine-trees extending their boughs to the Lord.

10/2/22

15
Remorphing

Remorphing of difeleth to lartife required
A bard that, by Ultimate Being inspired,
The favor of grace to requite had desired,
A bush that in burning the androgyne sired.

To wake in the morn as to Being new-made
The soul early born and with glory arrayed
In sweetest of meters had danced unafraid
That ever the energy-force be allayed.

The clapping of hands when the thunder one heard
The beat of the heart to extrinsecate stirred:
The rhythm within was prophetic, a bird
That sings ere the gift of the sun be conferred.

The song will be strong though the rhapsode should
    age:
In dithyramb antic and mantic the mage
With Miriam's timbrel and psalm would engage
The amorous hymn of the canticle sage.

10/1/22

16
Essential

Qur'an 15:26. Verily We created man of potter's clay of black mud altered, 27. And the Jinn did We create aforetime of essential fire.

A Portuguese poet, the greatest of all,
Was penning his epic when what should befall
But sudden extinction of light in the hall!
The candlelight vanished, he stared at the wall.

Then, turning bright eyes to the Master, his cat
Approached him ... The poet was thankful for that!
With light from the cat-eyes he'd write while he sat,
Nor ever a fright would he have to combàt.

Yet eyes of a feline will not extromit
A light—they are only reflectors of it.
The poet, how long he soever might sit,
Would gather no light, not the tiniest bit.

Well, such are the data that science may show.
But poetry tends to transcend, as we know ...
He might have beheld a mysterious glow.
To comfort the spirit in evident woe

A jinn who, created aforetime of flame,
Has means to illumine, a numen we name.
Imaginers view what few others might claim:
To aid him, a lumen conceivably came ...

10/2/22

17
Solomon

The canticle amorist chanted to me,
"My hymning recite, and your passion you'll free.
It powers the whole of the physical world:
My booklet is rightly begemmed and impearled.

'Twas Rabbi Akiba who lately declared,
The Lord of the Law for the Lover so cared,
Had Moses the Pentateuch never received,
The heart of the people need not be aggrieved

But rather could turn—as Sulamith had done—
To scriptures of love that the King had begun
When yearning, his thanks for the earth to express:
What doubled in value Sulamith would bless.

The taste of her kisses proved sweeter than wine,
For he in the breath of her love could divine
The dizzying flame which had galaxies whirled
When angels of grandeur their banner unfurled."

10/2/22

18
Receive

My coffee I haven't yet sampled—indeed,
What bread can most fully the passionate feed,
What wine might our craving most perfectly slake,
But poetry—wordsong the spirit can make?

I'm trusting an Abraham angel to come
And sing of re-seeding the garden wherefrom
When Adam and Eve had departed they yet
Would bear in the heart what they'd never forget.

'Tis fact that in bliss of the flesh and the blood
We tremble whenever a thundering thud
Of ocean primeval the strength will convey
That folk in their journey are showing the way.

The beat of the heart and the art of the beat
Are Solomon-wine than the heaven more sweet:
When bliss on a mountain of spices we find,
Sulamith is glad, and the passions are kind.

10/2/22

19
Hands

The map of the veins on an arm or a hand
A grownup could show might a boy-child command
To view with attention, admiring the sight
With plain fascination and quiet delight.

The rivers and streams and the currents of blue
On landscapes of life in their form and their hue
I truly admired and looked forward to see
What time transformations would happen to me.

Indeed they occurred, and I view them each day,
The mild elevations, the patterns that play
On palm and on forearm, on finger and wrist:
A wish is fulfilled and I nothing have missed.

While typing I watched them, the veins I described:
Has anyone pleasure more vital imbibed?
I've never yet heard in the verse of a bard
Such loving laudation of sight lucky-starred.

10/2/22

20
Songs

The songs—they keep coming: the writer who strived
Will feel he is hearing, "The time has arrived:
A while had you waited; at seventy-nine
Beneficent wealth is the honey you hived."

The Sufis their writing compared to the wine
That Noah had heartened: "No flood will confine!
The flask in my pocket is Ark Number Two:
Salvific the function to *that* I assign."

'Tis honey and wine and the Sabbath-bread: true
To heavenly purpose, my hymn will endue
An ardor encouraged and warmly averred:
Symposiast Plato and Rumi I view.

When particle-bundles of energy whirred
Surrounding the Throne of the King, they concurred,
Intoning: "Thrice holy, dear Lord, have we thrived,
New sounds who have fashioned to hallow the Word."

10/2/22

21
Rivers

The Rivers of Eden—could these be the veins
That bear all our manifold pleasures and pains
From heart of their birth to the worth one attains
When, writing a psalm, mind a holiness gains?

The Rivers are honey, milk, water, and wine:
They're life-giving nourishment, helping refine
The blessing of that which we sense, to align
The earth and the sky through the ears and the
    eyne.

The Rivers of Eden sing praise to the Sea,
Their heart, and the Source which for strivers will be
The force that empowered the Prophet, so he—
Aforetime on courser—disciples might free.

A steed pegasèan the pink and the gray
Of brain with the blue and the gold will array
When, Favor assisting the Breaking of Day,
We, sweven-ascending, a scripture will say.

10/2/22

22
Parable

Five poems I wrote. Then I had, as reward
(I'd better confess it), a sizable snack.
I napped, am refreshed, but my brain's feeling bored:
My sleep was too brief, and I suffer a lack

Of nutrient-energy, having forgot
Digestion takes time, and the nourishing strength
May fail till the deed is complete. I've been taught
Much food means a wait of inordinate length.

I fear I'm obliged to be idle some more
Until the return of the energy sought:
I hear the command, will be patient—a bore,
But maybe a vision will meanwhile be brought:

I'll hope for a dream, so that, wholly awake,
Both bloodstream and brain fresh resources will
    find:
New force from dormition I'll blissfully take;
A hymn will I sing, thanking body and mind.

10/2/22

23
Strange

How strange that I'm writing, how fine to have
    earned
The freedom to know there's a world to explore
Which, merely to think of, the soul may adore,
Since, watching my fingers while typing, I've learned

The magic of history, secrets profound
Of thought that is quite inconceivably deep,
Computer to make that my tributes will keep
And keyboard inviting my tunes to resound!

The marvels I tell are so recent that no
Diviner supposed how our progress would go,
But miracles come—when they wondrously grow

We cannot but sense we are favored by grace,
Unbounded and beating the heart, while we face
Our moment unfolding in time and in space—

What Grecian and Hebrew and Persian have taught
Inspiring, rewiring, reviving our thought.

10/2/22

24
Line

I'm writing in verse, but a "line" will transcend
Our usual thinking. 'Twill open, my friend,
Perspective. The Sufi, the Greek, and the Jew
Will deepen our hearing and widen our view.

A vertical stroke has the meaning "create."
'Tis *àliph* in Arabic. High the estate,
The station of knowledge we gain when we feel
The line in our heart is a heavenly seal.

It means "the beginning," the starting of things.
It also means "love," for the King of all Kings,
Inscribing it—hear from Hafeez!—in the heart,
Betokened both Love and Creation as Art.

Straight line for geometer Euclid had meant
A single and widthless dimension. Intent
On making the proof of each theorem pure,
Mere length, he had stated, alone would endure.

The lines in geometry textbooks are drawn
But clumsily. Breadthless, the ones whereupon
We gaze in the mind are ineffable norms
That hinted to Plato the heavenly Forms.

The Biblical God uttered, "Let there be light."
We heard, in a prelude foretelling our sight,

The words that were primal, primordial, first.
Our ears are awake; we're in hearing immersed.

Yes, "Let there be light" is a poetry line—
Longinus declared it sublime and Divine.
We see it and think of the heavenly Might,
But first had we *heard* it—and vanquished the night.

10/3/22

25
Steepled

Though hands may be folded or clasped in a pray'r
They equally well might be steepled. If so,
While fingertips meet, lifted upward in air,
A symbol we shape, that the spirit may grow.

The relevance here to the keyboard is brought,
Where halves come together at center in height;
An emblem to help us the tent will have taught:
Nomadic, prophetic, the soul feels a might.

The hands make a tent as the keyboard will do:
An Abraham-angel we patient await.
Then lift up your head, O ye gate! Let us view
The future in faith, and a posture made straight.

The hands and the stature, the keyboard and tent,
Preparing the heart for reciting a psalm,
I hope may call forth what the messenger meant:
Good news will come soon! We are gladdened, and
    calm.

10/3/22

26
Untitled

calligraphic painting by Shahid Alam

Creation and Chaos, however they fight,
Won't ruin our life: to the writer's delight
A harmony-will must continue in play
Renewed every dawn with the breaking of day.

A wave and a current, a surging of tide,
Pervading, astir, unabating abide;
Yet less than a threat can I feel it to be,
For equally songful and strong is the glee.

Each Arabic letter, a line or a curve
(More festive the better!), confining the swerve
The zebra-like stripes of the waves try to make,
Our thirst for a concord of pattern will slake.

The letters turn ribbons of holiday green;
Like buds of the holly are diamond-like seen
The cheer-bringing vowels to vocalize words—
With greenery-flourishes mindful of birds.

Occasional loops in the letters let through
The purest of white in a snowdrop for you;
The orange and green and the white bring to mind
The flowers of winter and make it more kind.

The delicate swells in the stripes white and black
Are animal-like; side and thigh, front and back,
They give me the sense of a creature that breathes
And power of life to the seër bequeaths.

Envision a present, a wrapping, a smile:
A Christmas-y feeling the mind may beguile.
Exuberant letters are seeking for speech
As we for the present so near to our reach.

10/3/22

27
Touched

Whenever my sugar-count number is low
And sales of my writings are pleasantly high,
A little bit crazy I'm tempted to go
And stand on a hilltop and shout at the sky!

The colorful gods who the strings of our fate
Control at the various ages we reach
Are playful—they're children! Let little and great
Indulge in their whimsy that none will impeach.

King David looked drunk when he danced by the
    ark;
For Noah the flask had been ark number two.
The moon riding high urges wolfhounds to bark,
And cats dash around in the room: hallelu!

When Rumi, more pious than many combined,
Envisioned the world as a round-dance of flame,
He sought out a partner; together they'd find
A scripture-tradition that angels acclaim.

10/3/22

28
Otis

The stretches you've done, best position to find,
Show comfort and health in relaxing, dear Cat.
The black and red blanket is aptly designed
For play and for deep satisfaction thereat.

Who looks at your portrait may gratitude feel
For glad benefaction. The care is ideal
Which you in your time of maturity get:
Let scene for a blest meditation be set!

The curves of the body, the thickly rich fur,
The white and the orange, the bliss of content
Are shown as the best of photographers meant.

We're thankful, together, to Sarah. By her
And Anna, who gave us the blanket, we're lent
A gift of great worth. All our friends will concur.

10/4/22

29
Workplace 1

Dear Sarah, how cheerful what autumn has done:
A scene that both office and mood will adorn
Allows you to work in a blossoming morn;
Some vines through the window sneak in, just for
    fun.

The red-turning maple-leaf—emblem of fall;
The pink-and-white bush and the flowering tree
Where blooms quite abundant are pleasing to see
Blend well with the orange-y bricks of the wall.

The office I worked in for thirty-five years
At Binghamton U. here in Vestal had faced
A widening alley for parking the cars.

A grass-covered hillside behind it had graced
The view with reminders that nature endears;
But lower the shades when the chrome-shining jars!

10/4/22

30
Workplace 2

*thanking my daughter Sarah and
my friend Michael Sharp*

I only just noticed, twin foliage wreaths
For windowpanes upper and lower appear,
Predestined to furnish a holiday cheer.
I focus on each as a mouth, and it breathes.

A viewer on facebook wrote only one word,
"Matisse," and by that was my memory stirred.
In tranquil museum a picture I see
Called "Dance of Rejoicing," a spring jubilee.

The wreaths in your snapshot seem dancing as well.
In snapjot, replying, made glad would I tell:
The leaves by the branches are held, as the arms
Of celebrant circlers are joined. To the charms

Of picture and photo and words would I sing:
Apollo and Bacchus and me—in a ring
You see us—now, Venus, hold hands with Matisse!
The spirit of Here finds, at last, a release!

10/4/22

31
Kafka 1

I'm reading the stories and entries, wherein
"Complete" and "unfinished" lack meaning. Begin
To write what we see's the procedure wherethrough
You get to know *me* while I get to know *you*.

For everything's dreamt. Country doctor, when
    called,
Will neither feel hopeful, excited, appalled,
Engaged nor made distant. No wound will appear.
Then suddenly, crawling with worms, it is here.

The horses that brought the physician were hid,
Stuffed thick in a pigsty. Through countryside rid,
Intrusively odd, through the windows they stick
Their heads, which are huge: is the kid really sick?

The doctor's required to head home, for the groom,
Who bit a girl's cheek, had been left in a room
Arousing a likelihood: soon will he chase
And capture the person he bit in the face.

The doctor is worried: Deceptive alarm?
Perverse to occur—only *helpers* to harm!
But *is* he assisting? We merely can say,
'Twas partly his fault he was called here today.

10/5/22

32
Kafka 2

"The Burrow," "The Mouse-folk" I long have
    postponed
Perusing. The prospect elicited groans:
I quailed at the burdensome weight of the jails
That bigotry builds when civility fails.

I tried "Little Woman" just now, and though late
It timely confirms what implacable hate
For no given reason, exuded in rage
Kept wordless, turned youth into withering age.

I know I'll continue the narrative works
That prove self-destructiveness lethally lurks
In crannies and cracks where the monsters emerge
When rulers encourage resentment to surge.

Franz Kafka, like me, was a Jew and a man,
A student of art, with a heart. When we scan
In Kafkian manner the strangest of dreams,
Be-loving embrace more available seems.

10/6/22

33
House

The "Drive" is called "Taylor"; the place where I live
Conditions for calm composition will give.
The moderate warmth and the quiet suffice
The Muse and the Sabbatine morn to entice.

The basement—front hall where my study you'll
    find—
The living-room, dining room, small kitchenette—
The bathroom and bedrooms, then, finely designed—
With attic—*five levels* create, to beget

A many-stage home for procession of thought,
With feeling of tone and of meter and line;
Great gift to a bard in rewirement they've brought
Who'll gladly to up-and-down travel incline.

The days of creation are six, and as well
The ways of our travel are sixfold. We tell
Habitually of the maps having four,
But myth and religion have furnished two more.

10/6/22

34
Bush 1

A bush that was burning yet never consumed
Had shone before Moses: the heart is illumed
By force of the fire that the passionate heat
Inspires in the mind that can feel it, so sweet.

The flame preternatural seems, but to me
The truly most natural emblem 'twill be
Of total perfection. Uniting desires,
The androgyne stands for com-passionate fires.

How brush-like and fluffy and tenderly branched
The filament-clustering bush! Blood unstanched
The ruddiest carmine of leaves in the fall
On colorful plant shouted passionate call.

On bodies of humans the bush will reveal,
In androgyne fashion, what none need conceal:
May puffy-curled beard be a sign of the same,
Designed by the manly and womanly Name.

10/6/22

35
Kafka 3

"The Burrow" and "Great Wall of China" no friend
Allow to appear, for the speaker's alone.
The kingdom or hollow of Fear will extend
Forever around the Damòclean throne.

The "foe from the Northland" no builder has kenned;
One's Being in fear turns Becoming to stone.
Invaders unviewed keep the Burrower penned;
The Wall's warding off the unseen, the unknown.

The Wall and Peking seem a cloud in the sky,
Not two things but one in a dream floating by.
The Digger a beast, or of whistlers a crowd
Envisions, unreal as the king-city cloud.

The burrow a Castle is called, but a Tomb
It might have been named. All the vastness of room
Amounts to a zero, for naught do we know!
The Emperor's dead—he lived ages ago.

10/6/22

36
Kafka 4

The voice in "The Bridge" tells directly that he
Himself is the bridge, and contented might be
If walkers their acts of aggression would cease.
They baffle the speaker and grant him no peace.

He's poked with a stick, an umbrella, who knows
What next it might be—a vexation that grows.
One dullard jumped up, booted feet—he will land
With strength, as if angry. One can't understand ...

The bridge, stomach downward, is eager to see
What kind of a creature that leaper might be ...
The way he's positioned he tries to reverse.
Things won't be improved; he is making them worse!

When halfway turned over, he'll suddenly fall—
A deathward descent that will readers appall.
The story is barely a paragraph long.
Its meaning I'll hint in the following song:

10/6/22

37
Kafka 5

Two sides of the river the Bridge to connect
Had tried—but the way wasn't wholly correct.
How better to serve, to unite the two sides?
I sought a solution, and yet it still hides.

The problem, I think, would be clearer, indeed,
If we in the *Diaries* rightly would read.
They richly are flavored with words that appeal
From Yiddish tradition, and uttered with zeal.

Rachmonës we hear, and *parnussë,* and more
Ethnicity-links; quite abundant, the store
Of lively impressions that Kafka enjoyed
That brave Jewish actors in Prague had deployed.

The Bridge, as a Writer, a problem would pose:
Could Jewish tradition be linked to the prose
That Kafka in German was writing? I think
The bridge had collapsed. We are lacking the link.

10/6/22

38
Kafka 6

But maybe I'm speaking too quickly? In fact,
The diary-work no alertness had lacked:
When pages are written in variant forms,
Might Kafka be seen to be seeking for norms

Of style that, revised, might successfully make
A well-crafted artwork? This volume I take,
As others have done, for a book we should read
To lend what our starved sensibilities need:

A tour of cafés, an attendance at plays,
Much fine entertainment the hearer will praise.
Companion Max Brod *Jewish Women* portrayed
And so an example for Kafka displayed

Of writing designed as a "bridge," I would think.
The personal nightmares of Kafka might "sink,"
He may have been wary of parables placed
With links too specific to haters he'd faced ...

10/6/22

39
Hands 2

My hands! Feel their blood that is rushing, as fit:
The heart that is beating! Just harken to it!
I've written of house and of nest and of bush:
Quick pounding gives thought a particular push …

A story I've read about heavenly "Hands,"
The name Sherwood Anderson favored, demands
A guide with a sensitive touch to reveal
How, wingèd, the fingers a singer may heal.

The veins are the bearers of Eden-blue stream;
I've treated this earlier—lovable theme!
In lyrics 19, 25 you will find
More hymns to the hand, with its glories divined.

The pinions, angelic, with messenger-bliss
Great speed will acquire in the dance when they kiss
The letters that wait on the keyboard to hear
The hymn they will raise when the fingers come
    near.

10/6/22

40
Computer

Though much of the planet with battles be rife,
Computer, sing sweetlier, give us more life!
Though sands of the desert be reft of a tune,
Computer, sing hymns, and deliver a boon!

If sugar count, book sales go up or go down,
Excite me, computer, make lighter the crown!
Should soul of the writer, once higher, sink low,
Enlighten, computer, the path where I go!

When loneliness total and tomblike might seem,
Refresh me, computer, with messenger-dream!
Though billions of people and galaxies roam,
Reboot me, computer, my help and my home!

The body and soul in a union must be:
Illumine, computer, the roadway for me!
Let writer and wonder-machine become one:
Be true, dear computer, to love till I'm done!

10/6/22

41
Tactics

Conversing with Kafka refreshes although
We're deeply immersed in a dream-tale of woe
Obsessive, depressive ... We're told that he laughed
While writing—for *my* part, I fear going daft!

A dialogue-tactic I thus recommend:
Consider your mentor a personal friend:
He's written a parable? Quickly respond
With one of your own, in a partnering bond.

Each comrade may patient and therapist be:
Not I and not you, but the blend that is *we*
Will something achieve with a form of its own
In shapes that from new comprehension have grown.

A journeyman-journaler opens a gate.
Our Abraham-angel we, heartened, await;
The birth he proclaims he will partially aid,
Babe warmed by the cordial announcement he made.

10/6/22

42
Kafka 7

Petition refused. In "Refusal" that's all
That happened. Such fate would petitions befall
Quite often, officials, gold-braided, recall.
Expected, predicted. There's naught to appall.

The ruler, Collector of Taxes, was not
Elected. Yet, humble, the subjects were taught
That habits of old are traditions well wrought
And not to be altered. So, perish the thought!

A version of China, its Wall filled with gaps—
We feel no alarm, should efficiency lapse.
The lip-server mouthpieces nothing can learn:
Strict ritual awe will authority earn.

A radio program: "Abortion, and guns,
And China—election integrity, too."
Of worshipful hate thus the litany runs:
The fascists are many, the democrats few.

10/6/22

43
Sudden

A lengthy, tall shadow the telephone pole
Had cast, that was hiding the rabbit from sight.
My walking through grass, unfamiliar, a fright—
At least an unease—had aroused, and the goal

Was now to escape a disturbance unknown.
He bounced down the slope of the hill on the lawn,
Efficient and quick, moving on, moving on—
With white-banner tail-fur quite palpably shown.

I liked it, and smiled, wouldn't laugh, didn't dare:
I rather would grant him a freedom from care.
Thick rain had just fallen; at two forty-two

A peaceable morning was offered to you:
Friend Rabbit, fast runner, your visit, though brief,
Amused me: don't trip on a slippery leaf!

10/7/22

44
Prayer

Contèmplative thought and petitioner's pray'r
Are one; the distinction will vanish in air.
I wait for the hint of a psalm, no request
In phrasing extended, but calm and at rest.

I sense it will come as a heaven-bequest:
Of hymns will the Spirit have plenty to spare.
I glance at the screen, but I needn't quite stare:
The quiet of night is a moon-lumen fest.

Two gifts of the Granter one cannot compare:
The sun let a cat bring the east to the west.
My breathing can widen my lungs and my chest

And thus will my heart for surrender prepare.
The Bride has arrived in her holiday best:
Sing gently, my soul; let the Sabbath be blest.

10/7/22

45
Preparation

The tongue moves around in the mouth to explore
How varying placement may stimulate sound.
Teeth, palate are walls, and we're moving around,
As if in a cave we'd not entered before.

The touching and tasting and testing of all
The surfaces made for production of tone
Expand the sensation spelunkers have known
While hearing the echoing summons, the call.

From languages learned in the past may return
Some feelings you think you may want to repeat:
The timbres are flavored: tart, sour, bitter, sweet.

My days are the pages the hearer will turn,
My head is the place where the organist plays,
My heart is the source of the craving to praise.

10/7/22

46
Notes

The doe that had nuzzled and nibbled and chewed
The foliage fragments and leaves of the grass,
While leisurely strolling, with pleasure I viewed.
So lovely a scene one need never let pass:

The face of the animal, calm and content,
A memory record requested of me:
I went to my writing machine, and we'll see
What further detail is for melody sent.

Full soon "mother's whistler" a message will lend
When water is heated and audibly steamed.
'Twill add to impressions afloat, semi-dreamed …

Remember the rumble and roar of the wheels
The roll-cart recycler engendered?—through air
A squirrel had flown—with what grace, and what
    flair!

10/7/22

47
Bibliomancer 1

Qur'an 42:13. He hath ordained for you that religion which He commended unto Noah, and that which We inspire in thee (Muhammad), and that which We commended unto Abraham and Moses and Jesus, saying: Establish the religion, and be not divided therein.

More joy to convey, as the ancients had done,
I choose for my purpose, and thus have begun
By opening scripture to see what I find,
And lo! here's a doctrine of many-in-one.

Diverse are the callings that Spirit designed,
A Love to convey that is wide, unconfined,
United not split, undivided in heart,
Benevolent, merciful, passionate, kind.

Full many the cups that are crafted with art,
Full many locales where a pilgrim can start,
Full many the depths where the gold may repose,
Full many the souls that their wisdom impart.

Muhammad and Jesus and Abraham chose
The thought that let Moses and Noah disclose
A daybreak of soul, and a dawning of sun:
Let nightingale sing to the heavenly Rose!

10/8/22

48
Bibliomancer 2

Song of Songs 4:16. Awake, O north wind; and come, thou south; blow upon my garden, that the spices thereof may flow out. Let my beloved come into his garden, and eat his pleasant fruits.

Come, nòrthwind, and O, you most beautiful south!
Blow spice-laden breeze! Let my darling his mouth
Refresh with the rarest of fragrance, and know
My love, like the springtime, will flourish and grow!

Our garden the emblem of living let be.
I opened the scripture, and what did I see
But that which in birds of the morning I hear:
A concord of comrades, to love and revere.

Our mother the earth and our father the sky
Are wedded forever: let poet descry
The wedding of soul to the Lord; by the grace
Of dawn-resurrection 'twill daily take place.

In psalming my thanks, I arising can feel
A faithful requital: a Solomon seal
Is pledging a depth, a devotion whereof
The source and the goal are our heavenly love.

10/8/22

49
Bibliomancer 3

Virgil, Fourth Eclogue:

*"Comes from the Sibyl Cumaean a song of the end of
an era: New generations we hear are beginning their
course more distinguished. Lady Astraea returns,
and the Golden Age, Saturn's dominion;
Soon from the heaven sublime will descend a new
birth of the people."*

The bibliomancers who Virgil revered
In verses like these found a message endeared.
"The life that the Child will receive" is our guide,
And "Over the peace of the world he'll preside."

A major event at the Emperor's court,
A wedding auspicious, inspired the report
A Sybil, an oracle, widely was thought
A message prophetic and wise to have brought.

For centuries writings of Virgil were used
As oracles, being by heaven infused
With meanings that Christ or Isaiah might seem
To echo and mirror a heavenly gleam.

In "yellow of saffron and ruddiest red"
The lambs will be clad who to meadows are led;

No Roman will labor, all creatures make peace;
No dye will be needed for native-hued fleece.

10/8/22

50
Biography

To morning that smiles I would make my reply:
"A fitting symbolical scene you display!
Entrancing, the deep, empathetical way
Biographer's love can a culture survey

And life led within it. You open the eye,
The mind and the heart, to an earth and a sky
All utterly new, and are bringing them nigh—
An epic, a novel, a lyric, a play.

Herr Stach, in your *Kafka*, we're sad and we sigh
But grace have we gained that we'll forward repay:
A lifegiving multi-directional way
Abandonment's dolor converted to day.

You're also new fragments unearthing—hurray!
They've often the rawness of dream, as you say ...
I asked, *while asleep*, 'Odd computer-glitch—why
Should stubborn delete-key all strikings defy?'"

10/8/22

51
Cat

We hear of our brevity—"nothing comes back."
Why's lesser longevity viewed as a lack?
And—lesser than what? than a cat? It is fall.
Let Moment be entered, encompassing all.

Consider the number of breaths that you take
Per hour, per year. Not a tremble or shake
You feel, in your mighty and perfect machine—
Your heart and your lungs, in their breathing
    pristine.

The end of your time's like the end of your space:
You alter them, changing your pace and your place.
In writing these words for the world to peruse
A hermit I'm not, who aloneness refuse.

That poems can lengthen your life we have heard;
We widen and deepen it too, with our word.
The soul's poemoment, in human and cat,
Is numen and lumen and rounded, not flat.

10/9/22

52
St(art)

The paper to start with advice column—fun!
Myself, with the comics I've often begun
Before the perusal of news took their place.
Good humor is "news" that events won't disgrace.

A poem a day will fresh mind-life begin.
Your feelings diurnal Greek urns may excel
By adding the beat to what leaf-legends tell.
With music and pictures high triumph you win.

"Some counsel for getting to Carnegie Hall?"
"Just practice, dear boy. Practice, practice is all.
The instrument mastered, each phrasing will fall
At once into place." Oh, divine! Standing tall,

I'm striding, whilst holding my dear violin
(My epipsychidion), hearing within
The hymns that are charming my carnegie way!
(I've practiced and practiced—a poem a day ...)

10/9/22

53
Awaking

My love for a comforting, motherly sleep
(This line just arrived, and I'm cherishing it,
For surely what comes will be perfectly fit)
I treasure: the pleasure life holy will keep.

I dream Sleeping Beauty—her pupil am I
(Forget about heroes of masculine mold
That rescue fair maidens, and castle-keys hold)
And know I will be till the day that I die.

Lips kissed with the taste of her honey, I lay
(Scant wakefulness having attained, and indeed
For decades or days I'd be failing to heed)
Enchanted, awaiting the blessing she'd say.

Dear Lady, the gift you entrusted to me
(Who yet had to journey at first through the realm
Abiding, of mind, having grasp of the helm)
Would bring me to hear, "Sing the hymn that will
    be."

10/20/22

54
Thracian

sculpture posted on Facebook by Charles Campbell

Saint Emperor Leo looks upward. A wise,
Encouraging spirit you see from his eyes:
The gaze that is searching looks inward as well;
In Greek, of the words he had heard will he tell.

His grand coronation the Eastern realm shows
A Christian adherence and fervor that glows.
The curls are arranged in what seems like a wreath:
Symmetrical order this lord will bequeath.

I readily picture his hands at the keys,
Where lyrical hymns he will fashion with ease:
I, too, looking inward-and-upward would write

The word of the heart and the thought of the height.
Let prudence and judgment inform and instill
Directly the strength of the heavenly Will.

10/10/22

55
Presentiments

A couple of times in my earlier years
Some hint was I given, at first of my fears
And then of my hopes, enigmatic and small,
And yet on mysterious depth did they call.

A couple of weeks or of months—who can say?—
Short, blurted, aborted—mere grunts—might one hear.
I never would speak—all the words went away ...
The grunts were a puzzle—and didn't endear!

Well, that was in grade school. Much later, full grown,
I started my humming: all day I would hum.
At times it would make my collocutor glum—
Please stop! Just remember, you're not *quite* alone!

The grunting, the humming, I think might have meant
I'd felt I had something to say or to sing ...
But no one the news of my mission would bring:
'Twould only be later that poems were sent.

10/10/22

56
Give

So long as a bird is permitted to sing
He'll not have a care for a critic's review.
The morning, rebirthing, his worth may renew
Far more than a crown on the pate of a king.

A crowd is an emblem, parental at best,
Mere progeny-laud. But is rental the test?
Applause and celebrity greedy to get,
The death of our freedom's the price we have set.

The Psalm and the Gospel of Beauty say, "Gift
You serve, not deserve. To the Giver pray lift
Your voices in joy and with gratitude dance,
Join mountain and fountain, the Granter enhance.

Preferment and worship no longer receive
The ones who in idols of pride would believe.
Your present is priceless, forget the receipt:
Than Solomon's wine make your lyric more sweet.

10/10/22

57
Timeful

Though timeless, the poem proved timeful to me.
'Twas filled with the time of its coming to be
With timefulness given to people who heard
How timelife had widened the sphere of the word.

When bursting with happiness time you may feel
Consists of the minutes that each are more real
When wealth of their being in musical swell
Of joy in creating a maker may tell.

The self the most famous creator was not
A maker yet named till the time was begot
When fruitfulness came because timefulness grew
With moments momentous becoming in you.

The poem that made me a maker I more
Awaitingly shaping the form would adore
While grateful with timefulness greater would fill
The shaker and shaper the waker the will.

10/10/22

58
Ranakpur

reply to a Facebook posting

This temple for Jains in the district Bharaht
A lesson on gains to the wise will have taught.
Said bold Ramna Kumbha, the donor of land,
"'Tis here, in my honor, a column should stand,

And make it impressive, gigantic in height!"
It rose in the daytime—but fell every night!
No reason, however, the builders had found
Why, over and over, 'twould fall to the ground.

Well, Ramna was clever. He smilingly sighed,
"Experience teaches me, 'Lessen your pride.'
The quelling of self, rampant ego to tame,
Had shown that extravagant posing's to blame.

Stop work on that pomp! You a temple should build."
So glad was the vast architectural guild,
One thousand four hundred and forty and four
The columns they lofted and loved him the more.

10/10/22

59
Windows

reply to Jaimee Wriston Colbert on Facebook

They haven't been washed since that morning of yore
When I was conscripted by Mother-in-law
To help with the cleaning. Her thought was, the more
The workers, the sooner we're done. And I saw

The logic of that. On the whole, though, because
My eyes to the light are quite sensitive, I
With curtain and blinds am observing the laws
Of guarding my sight, and some labor pass by.

The kitchen-and-dining-room layout of glass,
However, I keep unobstructed and clear.
The doe, fawn, and stag (how I love to watch deer!),
The robin, the chipmunk, the squirrel that pass

While willow wands heave and the maple leaves flare
And multi-directional breezes reveal
The vast panorama of dance in the air—
Such views for a poet are proving ideal.

10/11/22

60
Tech

The clunky nonfunctional printer they'd sent
At last had been (thankfully!) taken away!
A present they'd left me, relieved that today
The hall was uncluttered. With helpful intent

A sort of computer tutorial they
Included, explaining the nature of all
The recent improvements in cartridges. Call
Me slightly tech-challenged, but—strange, the array

Of colors appearing to vary the hues
Of red or magenta or pink (?) ... With a face
Of welcoming, smiling, pink-white, that would grace
A recipe book, she—delighted!—the news

Unfolded of nuance and delicate tints
And deeper expressions I didn't quite see
That switching my ink-brand provided for me.
Persuasive, the rhetoric, framed to convince.

I looked at the back of a cartridge and viewed
A cluster of outlets, all silver-gilt hued,
So many, so tiny—would *needles* fit in?
Would wires be required? Where to *find* them?
    Begin ...

10/12/22

61
Experiment

The meter so sweetly careens through my brain
You'll straightaway grasp ('twere a bore to explain)
Why now is the time an experiment swift
Grabbed hold of my thinking and coursed o'er the plain.

The rhymes will come quickly, my spirits to lift
(Blithe jocular mood there's no reason to shift)—
A fit or a seizure, carousal in sound,
Quite free of entreaty, bestowed as a gift.

The strophe of Omar, melodious ground
Of canorous action, an outlet has found
And comes at my summons with gratitude-gleam
For lyrical fountaining. Onward we're bound!

Requiring no pretext or topic or theme
Save speed in the race for the reader's esteem
By faith in the moment that none may constrain
Made lords of the Jordan we're fording the stream.

10/13/22

62
Schoolmaster

"It goes without saying" and "needless to say"
Are nonsense. Or else you are lying. Okay?
The money I've honestly, earnestly earned
Why spend to buy words that their author had
    spurned?

"Please hold: we'll be back momentarily." Oh?
You'll speak me to just *for a moment*? Why so?
If "back in a minute" you mean, say it plain.
Proud polysyllabic display is in vain.

The spelling "correctors" quite widely in use
Repetitive errors unwisely unloose.
"Impostor"—last syllable spelled with an "o"—
Means fraudster or scammer, as some of us know.

"Imposter"—hey guys, listen up, don't be lax—
Is one who will levy an impost, a tax.
Impostor, the fraud who is spelled with an "e"—
Bad software engendered ubiquitously.

10/13/22

63
Benefits

Improvements in health when you age? There are three
Rewarding my days, and quite fortunately.
Think back to your thirties—the pains unassuaged
From vascular headaches!—they left as I aged.

The weather—wet, chilly—demanded I wear
A bulky fur hat for combatting damp air.
The advent of advil helped out for some years ...
But, aches having gone, no more throbbing one fears!

Another great gift: no more classrooms (!) had meant
The toxic fluorescence of lights would relent!
Farewell to the redeye that nothing would cure.
Blest pleasure! Dim light in my home will endure.

And lastly, the trousers that dreadfully itched,
Though made out of cotton, were chemical-glitched
And torture accorded in youth, but today
They're painless—all allergies driven away!

10/14/22

64
Instructional

Instructional poems are blazoned in fame:
The *Georgics* by Virgil the merit might claim
Of offering help when you're running a farm.
De Rerum Natura the student may charm

As forming a textbook where readers will glean
A knowledge of atoms in space. The serene
Triumphant Lucretius had figured it out,
Informing the Romans what life was about.

To counter complaints that on Facebook I hear
Regarding the rigors of diet, some cheer
I'll offer—a meal diabetics will find
For taste and for health quite divinely designed.

Unfreeze a fine loaf of Ezekiel bread.
(4:9 is the scriptural verse where the grains
Are listed). And then on the toast you will spread
Some fresh basil pesto, with olive oil. Gains

Are added in pleasure and health if you try
Some blueberries—ripe, low-glycemic—that I
Enjoy with Ezekiel cereal. Too,
Low-calorie almond-milk's perfect for you.

10/14/22

65
Cholent

Sukkot at Chabad of Binghamton

A holiday lunch for the Sabbath and Feast
Of Booths (modern-ancient Thanksgiving) I had.
The food was perfection. Especially glad
I felt that traditions yet live. Not the least

Enjoyable one was a novelty, too:
I'd never partaken of "cholent" before!
Potatoes and beans and tomatoes, with more
Fine flavor well-seasoned, 'tis made with a view

To adding a dish that is warm even though
The Sabbath forbids any fire to be lit
For cooking. But starting the stove would be fit
Pre-sundown on Friday! The steady, mild glow

Persists on Shabbat and no *work* will be done
By lighting a flame. Just relax, and have fun!
A soul-food for Jews! Kindly forebears of mine,
I honor your spirit, your tasteful design!

10/16/22

66
Shadows

Qur'an 16:48. Have they not observed all things that Allah hath created, how their shadows incline to the right and to the left, making prostration unto Allah, and they are lowly? 49. And unto Allah maketh prostration whatsoever is in the heavens and whatsoever is in the earth of living creatures, and the angels (also), and they are not proud.

It's morning and, filled with a being-alive,
I want to sing thanks for the writerly-drive
That says to me daily, Please dream up a hymn
To aid in my prayer for ways I may strive!

My fingers are eagerly dancing with vim;
My brain in the streaming of strive-life aswim;
New patterns of rhythm I feel in my feet;
New versions of Eden in vision to limn.

The gift amphibrachic tetrameter beat
Accords will wing forward my melody sweet
While, writerly-drive, you in shadow-form say,
Bow down like the grasses when breezes are fleet!

With gratitude playful, fit servants are they,
By flexible shadowing showing a way
Of heeding our wind-breath, in rising and dive,
In bending the soul to a heavenly sway.

10/17/22

67
Scripture

Of themes preternatural, seekers inquire,
"When things viewed unclearly I feel the desire
More keenly to see and at last understand,
How best might I gratify such a demand?"

Well, whether a god's in existence or not
May well matter less for the health of your thought
Than seeking what's greater than "ego" or "me":
Your human imagining strive to set free!

I find it a comfort that scriptures exist.
And what are they good for? Whatever you've missed
By fearing for selfhood and fostering pride
You'll partly "fill in" with a possible guide.

Just open a wisdom book: I the Qur'an
Find rich in what fortune may offer: a dawn
May gleam, and a seed, inadvertently sown,
To flourish may soon have assurgently grown.

10/17/22

68
Message

"I hope you've been well, haven't recently heard.
Then—just a few days ago—gee, what a dream …
It seemed we were younger. From sun's autumn
 gleam
We'd gone to a forest by wind-breath bestirred.

We played—we were jumping from moss-covered rock
To moss-covered rock. And we laughed and we
 laughed.
Your eyes were clear-focused, direct; we would talk—
Quite dark was your hair (you'd no beard, though).
 Your craft

Of poems would wait—we were having such fun!
It's great just to tell it—I loved it …" Soon done,
The letter, but—oh, I have got to include
The end—"Best time ever!"—how blissful the mood …

10/17/22

69
Marigolds

response to an e-mailed photo

Who'd ever have thought that, in spite of their name,
They all of the shades of their gold would transcend
And make a broad spectrum their multiple friend
And add to the tones with a bordering frame?

Soft burgundy petals an edging so thin
Of yellow possess that it might have been sewn.
Here, sprouts in a tender magenta have grown
Gold-clustered, competing your favor to win.

A crinkled and crumpled collection of white
Adds drama to mauve with an outburst of light.
The basket of wickerwork woven will play

In yellow-white-tan with the blossom array.
Each bluey-green aperture, too, interweaves
A hue-contribution with marigold leaves.

10/17/22

70
Refrain

Qur'an 19:76. [...] the good deeds which endure are better in thy Lord's sight for reward, and better for resort.

Remembrancer wise be the holy report:
Good deeds which endure will be better by far
Than those which more slight and forgettable are.
The best for reward and the best for resort

Are deeds that, like trees in the heavenly court
Stretch, prayerful, arms to the northerly star.
The best for reward and the best for resort
Are perfect in heart that no weakness can mar.

The path to the Lord may no obstacle bar.
The best for reward and the best for resort,
Enclosing the temple, victorious fort,
Good deeds, to the just, will be doors wide ajar.

The best for reward and the best for resort
Are homeward-bound boats that arrive at their port.

10/17/22

71
Chatinyan 2

bouquet posted on Facebook

His modes of approaching a painting are two.
Vase, table, brash dabs—light and dark in their blue.
But under cerulean coverlet you
Thin streamlets of paint—ultra-realist—view.

The baby's-breath, tiny her petals and white,
Dense-clustered carnations and marigolds bright—
Such true-life exactitude brings me delight,
Each vine—shady, sunny—shows camera-might.

On cups that are bulbous, of orange-y tints,
The strokes of the brush may be seen. To convince
The eye it is dreaming, they stem from a black
And purple amassing. Look far to the back,

Above the round berries, at orange and red
And yellowy strokes—we are growingly led
To find that expressive applyings of hue
To micro-detail are in visionscape wed.

10/17/22

72
Recompense

Qur'an 73:20. [...] Whatsoever ye send before you for your souls, ye will surely find it with Allah, better and greater in the recompense. [...]

Kind deeds, sent ahead for the health of your soul,
By heavenly recompense better are made.
And thus every hymn that the angels unlade,
Received and reshaped, more celestial a goal

Attains in the great compensation above.
Good acts move ahead, they are songful: a psalm
For neighbors outspread will their spirit-life calm
As hearts 'neath a coverlet soften with love.

Think well of your neighbor. We're standing before
Our fellow creations. Just open your door:
An Abraham-angel high tidings will bear

To each who is eagerly welcoming there.
Receive—and pay back, or pay forth, I should say:
Be Cleaver of Daybreak. Yourself be the Day.

10/18/22

73
Pumpkin

It suddenly struck me, the pumpkins I see
In so many pictures by Wyeth can be
The emblems of him, and conceivably me:
They're something unwinding in mind, and I'm free.

They grow in a place that is barren and dry
Below what may seem an unmerciful sky:
They've sunlight inside, that the cold may deny
Yet also can challenge the gold to defy.

Pure Being is round, old Parmenides claimed:
The pumpkin is, too; and the Ninety-nine-Named,
The Cleaver of Daybreak, the high and unblamed,
Has brought Itself nigh, as by dawn-ray inflamed.

The orange is kin to the heavenly blue—
And this, Andrew Wyeth finds mystical too:
He'll jacket or jeans, tub or bucket, endue
With something supernal, a comfort to view.

10/18/22

74
Diversity

Qur'an 49:13. O mankind! Lo! We have created you male and female, and have made you nations and tribes that ye may know one another. Lo! the noblest of you, in the sight of Allah, is the best in conduct. Lo! Allah is Knower, Aware.

Lo! female and male, and ye nations and tribes!
Come, know one another! The soul that imbibes
True empathy-wisdom, delectable wine
From river of Eden, feels friendship divine.

For God's in our knowledge: the creatures endear
Themselves to each other by loving. 'Tis clear
That wise com-prehend-ing implies an embrace!
Each countenance loved is the Heavenly Face.

Our friendship is noble: companions, the best
Of mentors, commend a symposial fest
Where lovers and comrades and sweethearts combine
Their hearts in a choiring, desires to align.

Lo! female and male, and ye nations and tribes!
Reverberant vastly in valleys, the vibes
Of sky-rising chorus in glorious hymn
The form of the Lord in the heavens can limn.

10/18/22

75
Sphere

Qur'an 5:16. [...] Allah guideth him who seeketh His good pleasure unto paths of peace. He bringeth them out of darkness unto light by His decree, and guideth them unto a straight path.

From fighting to peace, and from darkness to light,
The Highest who seek will be guided aright.
Your prayer, entreaty, thanksgiving, or song
Straight pathway will take to the heavenly throng.

Our spherical planet ensures that the gate
To heaven is everywhere. Paths will be straight
If journeys along them be headed for height:
Illumining Love's All-encompassing Might.

Newtonian science made "up" obsolete;
The life-drive had caused it a prior defeat:
The world of the spirit is one and entire,
An infinite realm of unending desire.

A sea without shore is our lady-and-lord:
We rose from the Ocean to One we adored.
Let sacred arithmetic fruitfulness be:
Add one to the One and the two become three.

10/18/22

76
Squirrel 1

One squirrel? That's *all* you have chosen for theme?
'Tis more than sufficient for Aesop-esteem.
No creature has more amphibrachian speed
To give us a hint about heating, indeed!

The chill (late October) grows daily more brisk;
Diminutive rodents are facing a risk:
Yet powerful energy kindled within
A training permits that will victories win.

"Velocipede," meaning "fleet-footed" in Rome,
Though used to mean "bike," I'll bring closer to
    home.
I'll newly apply the imaginal root
To pick a describer that squirrel may suit.

To cultivate speed is to generate heat!
Our lightning-bolt rodent a dexterous feat
Of warmth-engineering achieves. Let him run!
One loud, final cheer!—and our lyric is done.

10/18/22

77
Similitudes

Qur'an 30:58. Verily We have coined for mankind in this Qur'an all kinds of similitudes; and indeed if thou camest unto them with a miracle, those who disbelieve would verily exclaim: Ye are but tricksters!

Similitude, emblem, and parable coin
The teachers of poetry. Intellect join
To feeling, imagining, dreaming, and We
Reward will disperse that you, learning, will see.

A miracle's not an exception to laws
Of nature, where rules have a lifegiving cause.
The world that's around you will wonders reveal
When, filled with Our love, every sense you unseal.

A trickster may speak of the magical means
By which are presented his "miracle" scenes;
But who prestidigitates better than all?
The sleight-of-hand clown who will have a slight fall.

A symbol, a fable, a metaphor—they
Resemble a myth, a religion, and play
The role of a vessel, a glass, or a cup
That water of spirit may offer. Drink up!

10/18/22

78
Journey

Qur'an 84:16. Oh, I swear by the afterglow of sunset,
17. And by the night and all that it enshroudeth,
18. And by the moon when she is at the full,
19. That ye shall journey on from plane to plane.

When sunset is vanished, the afterglow left
Is thought staying on, while unfailing in heft:
When memory's deep we are granted a gift
Of Past Undiminished, that spirit can lift.

The night and the feeling of all it enshrouds
Are clarity, keenness, no kinship with clouds:
The dark is not Nil but a nourishing Nile,
Replete with potential of content and style.

How tender and gentle the moon at the full:
A sun re-envisioned in coolness, 'twill pull
The night-waking senses to see and to say
Enigmas that mind will interpret by day.

We travel from station to station, from plane
To plane through stages of space, to attain
Increasing awareness of what is unknown
Unless when conveyed to the Dreamer Alone.

10/18/22

79
Squirrel 2

Another fine fable has sprung into mind:
The squirrel, by burying food in the fall
May find it in spring—fitting payback for all
The hiding it did, for retrieval designed.

At times may a squirrel re-bury a seed
Or acorn or nut when he sees it secure.
The memory, strengthened, may also assure
The food wasn't thieved—that can happen, indeed!

Aesopian "moral" we now may employ:
Our poets a squirrely strategy show
By stashing loved moments away, for they know
Works newly re-found mean restoral of joy!

Computer, your memory-files may regale
The bard with a singular lyrical tale
Or psalm to re-read while he coffee imbibes
And moments well-cherished in heart re-inscribes.

10/19/22

80
Solace

Qur'an 94:1. Have We not caused thy bosom to dilate,
2. And eased thee of the burden
3. Which weighed down thy back;
4. And exalted thy fame?
5. But lo! with hardship goeth ease,
6. Lo! with hardship goeth ease;
7. So when thou are relieved, still toil
8. And strive to please thy Lord.

A sura or chapter Qur'anic I chose
Because of the wisdom and beauty endowed
By melody's depth which the spirit allowed
The hymn to re-sing while the sentiment glows.

One hundred fourteen are the cantos or parts
Contained in this book. As the volume proceeds,
The sections are briefer. In "Solace" one reads
A chapter complete, graced with lyrical arts.

Our lungs and our heart will expand while we strive
More space to provide where the Lord may come in.
Still breathing more deeply, to chant we begin:
May grace of the High bring our writing alive!

In serving the life-drive both labor and rest
Abundantly come, twinning hardship and ease.

By framing my psalm, deeper Power to please,
I pray that my effort by This will be blest.

10/19/22

81
Newspaper 1

story caption: 'A retirement home for cats'
in Afton (NY)

The *Press & Sun-Bulletin* (Tuesday) displayed
A photo I really don't want to discard.
So cozily warm, it appeals to the bard:
A snuggle-and-cuddle of cats it portrayed.

An animal, aging, more care will require.
My daughter's cat Otis, who's orange and white
And clever and likeable, lending delight,
And whom we've had many fine years to admire,

Quite frequent injection of saltwater needs
To help him make up for a sodium lack.
The lady in Afton (who lauds "giving back")
Dear cats—twenty-five of them—cares for and feeds.

Three cats in the photo remind me of those
I saw on a shelf in a barn, all entwined
In sleepy-time amity. Thus, one may find,
A welcoming, loving mentality grows.

10/19/22

82
Newspaper 2

advice column heading: To expectant mom,
'makes no sense'
the father should be in delivery room ("Ask Carolyn")

"No spectator sport!" cries the mom in dismay.
Both sister and mother are willing to aid,
So why should the husband objections have made?
Is Mom in the right when she sends him away?

Said Carolyn, "No. She must *not* underplay
How treasured, how cherished the moment will be
When Dad his miraculous baby will see!
How sad, in the 'waiting room' having to stay! ..."

When Sarah was born, I had learned my Lamaze;
His coaching technique should elicit hurrahs!
My wife, though, a woman of patience and mirth,
Had understood perfectly how to give birth:

So wisely aware and so calm did she prove,
The baby would quite expeditiously move.
Dear Sarah's loud cry was so wondrous to me
No music more glorious ever could be!

10/19/22

83
Better

Qur'an 41:34. The good deed and the evil deed are not alike.
Repel the evil deed with one which is better [....]

Bad deeds to defeat, a good action is best.
An act that seems bad, with a fine one replace.
Wolves claw and retaliate. People, show grace!
Kind smiles are commended by holy behest.

The life-drive is everywhere—sacred the Face.
The star in the east and the star in the west
Are both of them Venus, the Beauty, the blest ...
Let souls to please Deity speedily race.

May mindfulness-life be a gratitude-fest.
Watch tree-boughs in love with their friends
    interlace.
We love what is deathless, what naught can erase;
By helping your friend earn a Sabbatine rest.

Write holiest lines, with a heavenly trace.
Be ardent in welcoming birds to your nest.
Let breaths give you lung-strength and widen your
    chest.
Pray welcome your fellows with fervent embrace.

10/19/22

84
Guarded

Qur'an 75:19. Nay, but those who disbelieve live in denial
20. And Allah, all unseen, surroundeth them.
21. Nay, but it is a glorious Qur'an.
22. On a guarded tablet.

When Gabriel ordered Muhammad to read
(Though reading was something he'd never been taught)
At first had the Prophet been doubtful. He thought,
How might I comply with this duty, indeed?

He read it, however. A miracle wrought
By heavenly force had allowed him to heed
The Godly command, whereof worlds would have need.
A Mystery lent him the skill that he sought.

What sort of a document, then, had he read?
On parchment, or bronze? Or on paper, or stone?
The scripture no answer has given. Instead,
He likely perused what the Spirit alone

Allowed him to read, gave him strength to begin
To learn of the Universe, looking within.
A tablet well-guarded, inviolate, pure!
The depth of your soul will its value ensure.

10/19/22

85
Hollowed

*A stair not deeply hollowed out by footsteps is, from its own point of view,
merely a lackluster assemblage of wood.*

—*Franz Kafka, Aphorism 59, tr. by Rainer Stach in*
The Aphorisms of Franz Kafka
(*Princeton UP 2022*)

As Kafka's a hiker, his metaphor trove
May feature a place where a person might walk.
A hollowed-out stair's like a writer whom talk
And gesture and friendship made happy to rove,

Or maybe a pathway that leads through a grove
Where oaks are a-rustle with hints from the air …
Familiar, the creak of the deeply-loved stair,
More cozy, well-warmed by the wheezy old stove.

Some decades of reading it took me to learn:
For lustre of wood you must craft and create.
Each poem I write is a place where I turn

And, looking around, feel the bliss one may earn
Remembering warmth which no years may abate …
O staircase of childhood, to you I return!

10/19/22

86
Played

Your own violin, when more frequently played,
More sweetly, you feel, is caressing the phrase
You shape: 'tis a friendlier spirit that plays
In union with you. Souls together are made

More sensitive, each, to the other-desire.
An altering pressure will mean that the bow
More ardently sings; and, with motion more slow
If, yearning for passion, you deeply aspire,

The strokes will more tenderly, softlier flow.
Vibrato, with delicate wavelength, is heard
As if it were formed by a deep-meaning word:
The arm, by its rising and falling, will show

The breathing, *bel canto,* the A and the O.
Two partners in heart-love to heaven will go.

10/19/22

87
Barrett

Come all you bold heroes, give ear to my song
I'll sing in the praise of good brandy and rum

—by William Alexander Barrett, 1891,
posted on Facebook by Jeff Bronfeld

"Come all you bold heroes, give ear to my song:
I'll sing in the praise of good brandy and rum."
I'm not a big drinker but join in the throng
To hear amphibrachic tetrameter thrum.

Let's relish our life, as it doesn't last long:
Like wind will we go, as like water we've come.
Suggest me a ping and I'll counter with pong:
Reluctant to add, you'll subtract from the sum.

Farewell to my meekness; re-label me strong:
You don't know the words? Doesn't matter, just hum.
Play tabret and timbrel and cymbal and gong:
The ceilidh's complete with a bodhran for drum.

Good wishes to all; special aid to Hong Kong:
"Give freely, don't hoard" is the best rule of thumb.
To bells that go ding just reply with a dong:
With fish and some chips you feel chipper—yum yum!

10/19/22

88
Proverb

"The good ain't forever; the bad ain't for good."
The proverb, I think, will be well understood.
So long as you've tried just as hard as you could,
You're cool as a Druid while knocking on wood.

The saying was sent to my parents one day.
A funeral home, with a penchant for play,
A wit that is nimble would fondly portray,
Observing the rules of good taste, let us pray.

Some sprightly, fine humor will have the effect
Of aiding the aged who smiles may neglect;
Lest happier balance be threatened or wrecked,
A well-written adage your brain might protect.

"A thing that's worth doing is worth doing well."
A proverb of heaven? Well, here's one of hell:
"A thing that's worth learning great error is worth."
Good workers will heed it, preserving their mirth.

10/19/22

89
Ruminations

My home's near Chabàd, as you've probably guessed.
What's one of the things that I'm liking the best?
The question that comes, with precipitate glee:
What theme will the focus of Senior Group be?

We meet for discussion, with cookies and tea.
My question just heightened the sense of a fest:
Surprises are always a pleasure for me
Who feel like an honored and privileged guest.

September's chief topic—the nature of pray'r—
Was prime for a poet. No burden I bear
While writing, but rather the feeling I'll find
A reason for hymning, a psalm pre-designed.

The motion of walking—far brisker the air
Today, in October—seems nicely aligned
To raise my awareness of freedom from care:
Bright leaves in their triumph enlighten the mind!

10/20/22

90
"Otumnal"

Dear Jeremy, Sarah, the photo is great!
The orange-y stripes and the snowy pure white
Have led to a portrait suffused with the light
Dispersed on the leaves of the fall. We conflate

The brown and the umber and russet and tan—
The foliage-tones and the hues of the cat—
And deeply are pleased with the ensemble that
They make with the tree-leaves of green. When we
    scan

The picture we think, As he washes a paw
He's likely considering things that he saw
And scented and touched on the dampened, soft
    ground.

The calm, the tranquillity—these are profound.
My verbal translation I here will conclude:
Dear Otis, we're sharing your fall-loving mood!

10/21/22

91
Sappho

reproduction posted on Facebook

More helpful than statues of marble to me
Are portraits like this that we find in Pompeii:
A realist Roman depiction will play
With moments, informal, revealing, and free.

She's thoughtful and confident, focused and calm;
The end of her pen-handle touching her lips,
She waits for the Muse to deliver some tips:
The inward and outward unite, as in AUM,

Where AH is external and OOH turns within,
While M will smooth out any conflict. Begin:
You're holding a notebook, you're ready—the themes

Will vary, as ever in vigilant dreams.
I'm liking the curls in your lively coiffure:
In memory long may this image endure!

10/21/22

92
Half-awake

A slap in the face? You're unflinching. Keep cool
(Imperial Austro-Hungarian Rule).
Woke slowly from napping, and what did I find?
A sleep-fostered text with its meaning entwined.

There's no one more highly belauded—indeed,
The Kafka translations have tripled. I heed
The "gold rush" announcement and, hypnotized, read
What sounds in a reverie-poetry screed.

No writer need ever again be afraid
To follow directions and subject be made
To thoughts that the fairytale writerly gift
Might fail, quite entirely, one's spirits to lift.

For Kafka thus pondered, and worried, and stewed
And lived through what horrors, predicted, ensued
But hundreds of pages with candor yet penned,
And thus, my dear Franz, I am calling you Friend.

10/22/22

93
Prima

One style—*alla prima*—delights me these days.
I'm joining the site—it excites you to praise.
Skilled painters, who labor for just a few hours,
Respect will engender for zen-tending pow'rs.

Young girl—so convincing, the flesh tender-hued
(Paint thickly applied). Her expression I viewed
While startled by all of the light—face and eyes;
Firm muscle construction—to height you arise.

A sudden impasto incursion will give
Quick hints—iridescent, fluorescent—that live!
At times will the paint by the brush be laid on
In ways that awake you—the daybreak, the dawn.

In Mher Chatinyàn the technique, when applied
Together with micro-detail, can provide
Finesse neatly blended with Pollocky splash:
A fairytale magic with softness—and dash!

10/23/22

94
Bush 2

I'm Martin, and Musa, and Moses—Moshèh.
I'm facing a Sufi both present and past.
We speak, in my dream, about facts that will last:
"Eh'yeh," said the flame, and "ashèr," and "eh'yeh."

I am what I am—or *I'll be what I'll be.*
The bush that was burning but never consumed,
With utterance twofold in Hebrew, illumed
Both present and future when speaking to me.

The life-giving doubly significant Voice
Obrumpent and calming, will make you rejoice.
The Ultimate Being, the trumpet—It speaks

Of Now and the Future. Life *is* what It seeks.
The meanings are blended. I hear and I see:
I'll be what I am, and I am what I'll be.

10/24/22

95
Bush 3

If bushes that flame are a heaven-design
The clusters of hair that we sprout are divine.
If God is a bush that forever will burn
Examine yourself and of love you may learn.

If heat unconsumed should continue to be
'Tis rapt in an energy people can see.
If tendril or filament, thicket or strand
Arise from our bodies, we love understand.

If God and a man and a woman I view
When feeling the metaphor piercingly through
"I am what I am, and I'll be what I'll be,"
Says Flame, "Be ye grateful, dear Musa, to me."

Ablaze with the fire of impassioned consent,
A bush that is burning was certainly meant
To glorify love for the pilgrim in quest—
Be thanked, O dear Lord, for the hair on my chest.

10/24/22

96
Proverbs

Opposition is True friendship.

—*William Blake, Plate 3,* The Marriage of Heaven and Hell (1790)

From the true opponent, boundless courage flows into you.

—*Franz Kafka, Aphorism 23, tr. by Rainer Stach in* The Aphorisms of Franz Kafka *(Princeton UP 2022)*

"Opponent" makes energy rapidly flow.
It fills the creator, lets poetry go
Unhindered, unhampered, until one is filled
With joy that—"Friend" absent—one never could know.

Opponent, or Friend, is an energy source.
We need con-verse-ation to lend us the force
Explorers will sportively, thankful acquire
To heighten the mood that will grant our desire.

Without contrariety, how to progress?
A frenemy stirs you more greatly, not less
Than merely a mirror would do. We're instilled
With rivalry-drive that our effort will bless.

"Negations" that aim to destroy cannot aid.
But "Còntraries" help us. We grateful are made,
As Blake had explained and as Kafka had shown:
Such còntraries mean I'll be never alone.

10/24/22

BOOKS OF ORIGINAL AND TRANSLATED VERSE
BY MARTIN BIDNEY

Series: East-West Bridge Builders

Volume I: *East-West Poetry:*
A Western Poet Responds to Islamic Tradition in Sonnets,
Hymns, and Songs
State University of New York Press

Volume II: J. W. von Goethe, *East-West Divan:*
The Poems, with "Notes and Essays": Goethe's
Intercultural Dialogues
(translation from the German with original
verse commentaries)
State University of New York Press

Volume III: *Poems of Wine and Tavern Romance:*
A Dialogue with the Persian Poet Hafiz
(translated from von Hammer's German versions,
with original verse commentaries)
State University of New York Press

Volume IV: *A Unifying Light: Lyrical Responses*
to the Qur'an
Dialogic Poetry Press

Volume V: *The Boundless and the Beating Heart*
Friedrich Rückert's The Wisdom of the Brahman
Books 1–4 in Verse Translation with Comment Poems
Dialogic Poetry Press

Volume VI: *God the All-Imaginer:*
Wisdom of Sufi Master Ibn Arabi in 99 Modern Sonnets
(with new translations of his Three Mystic Odes,
27 full-page calligraphies by Shahid Alam)
Dialogic Poetry Press

Volume VII: *Russia's World Traveler Poet:
Eight Collections by Nikolay Gumilev:
Romantic Flowers, Pearls, Alien Sky, Quiver, Pyre,
Porcelain Pavilion, Tent, Fire Column*
Translated with Foreword by Martin Bidney
Introduction and Illustrations by Marina Zalesski
Dialogic Poetry Press

Volume VIII: *Six Dialogic Poetry Chapbooks:
Taxi Drivers, Magritte Paintings, Gallic Ballads,
Russian Loves, Kafka Reactions, Inferno Update*
Dialogic Poetry Press

Volume IX: *A Lover's Art: The Song of Songs in Musical
English Meters, plus 180 Original Love Poems in Reply—
A Dialogue with Scripture*
Dialogic Poetry Press

Volume X: *A Hundred Villanelles, A Hundred Blogatelles*
Dialogic Poetry Press

Other Poetry Books by Martin Bidney

*No Lovelier Melody Ever Was Known: A Month of
96 Poems in Amphibrachic Tetrameter Catalectic
(9/23/22–10/24/22)*
Dialogic Poetry Press

*Asclepiad Explorer: Ninety-nine Poems and Four Songs
(7/15/22–9/17/22)*
Dialogic Poetry Press

*More Four! Four Beats, Four Lines, Four Stanzas;
Three Hundred Four Wordsongs*
Dialogic Poetry Press

Alcaic Adventurer: Ninety-nine Poems and Five Songs (5/16/22–7/10/22)
Dialogic Poetry Press

High Five!—The William Shakespeare Beat Is Back! Four Hundred Newly Written Poems Prove it!
Dialogic Poetry Press

Book of the Heaven Eleven: A Rhythm Pattern for Three Months of Turning Difeleth to Lartife, with Blogatelles
Dialogic Poetry Press

The Heart of Giordano Bruno: New Poems Interpreting Highlights of His Book "The Heroic Enthusiasms"
Dialogic Poetry Press

Modern Psalms in Ancient Rhythm with Brief Commentaries in Verse and Prose
Dialogic Poetry Press

Persian Poetic Renaissance: Lyrics by Fifteen Sufi Poets in "Verse Interviews"
Dialogic Poetry Press

Shi-Jing, or Book of Songs: China's Earliest Verse Anthology rendered into German by Friedrich Rückert, form-faithfully translated by Martin Bidney
Dialogic Poetry Press

Owed to Omar: Adventures with a Persian-style Quatrain—100 Original Poems with Blogatelles (A Talk-show Interview Format)
Dialogic Poetry Press

Alexander Pushkin's Verse Novel Eugene Onegin *A Form-True Dialogic Verse Translation with Lyrical Replies and Supplements including a Dialogic Introduction with Caryl Emerson*
Dialogic Poetry Press

*Wordsongs of Jewish Thought: One Hundred Eight Tanya
Response Poems by Martin Bidney
Lyrical replies to passages in a classic work of Kabbalah
as presented in a three-volume edition with definitive
commentary by the world's foremost authority on the
work, Rabbi Adin Steinsaltz*
Dialogic Poetry Press

*The Eclogues of Virgil, Ancient Roman Country Poems in
Their Original Rhythm, with Dialogue Replies in Verse
(Talk Show Interview Format)*
Dialogic Poetry Press

*Indian, Persian, Arabian Poetic Treasures
Form-Faithfully Rendered from Friedrich Rückert
with Dialogue Replies in Verse*
Dialogic Poetry Press

*Six Beat Sonnet Treats
Intricate, Elegant Gifts for You*
Dialogic Poetry Press

*Metamorphoses and Me
Interviewing Ovid: From Genesis to Apocalypse in 80
Sonnet Dialogues with an introductory memoir poem, The
Wordsong Interview: How a New Kind of Writing Arose*
Dialogic Poetry Press

*A Music Lover's Art: Wordsongs About Musical Compositions
Fourth Journal in Verse*
Dialogic Poetry Press

*Sufi Lyrics in the Egyptian Desert
Ninety Poems in Modified Omar Quatrain Form*
Dialogic Poetry Press

*The Rumi Interview Project: Ninety-nine Poems
from the* Methnewi
*Form-faithfully Translated from the Lyrical Versions
of Tholuck with Original Sonnet Replies*
Dialogic Poetry Press

*Book of the Dactyl: Third Journal in Verse
Including Poem-Dialogues with the Witty Mystic
Angelus Silesius*
Dialogic Poetry Press

*Book of the Anapest: Second Journal in Verse
A Feast of Word Song, with Notes*
Dialogic Poetry Press

*Book of the Amphibrach: First Journal in Verse—
A Feast of Word Song, with Notes*
Dialogic Poetry Press

*Book of the Floating Refrain: Tone-Crafted Poems
with Blogatelles*
Dialogic Poetry Press

*Bliss in Triple Rhythm—A Toolbox for Poets: Nine Ways to
Shape a Word Song Shown in 300 Original Poems*
Dialogic Poetry Press

*A Treat Not Known Before:
German-American Poetic Dialogues in Ancient Rhythms*
Martin Bidney / Phlipp Restetzki
Dialogic Poetry Press

*Rilke's Art of Metric Melody: Form-Faithful Translations
with Dialogic Verse Replies. Volume One:
New Poems I and II*
Dialogic Poetry Press

*A Hundred Artisanal Tonal Poems with Blogs
on Facing Pages:
Slimmed-down Fourteeners, Four-beat Lines,
and Tight, Sweet Harmonies*
Dialogic Poetry Press

Shakespair: Sonnet Replies to the 154 Sonnets
of William Shakespeare
Dialogic Poetry Press

Alexander Pushkin, *"Like a Fine Rug of Erivan"*:
West-East Poems
(trilingual with audio, co-translated from Russian and
co-edited with Bidney's Introduction)
Mommsen Foundation / Global Scholarly Publications

Saul Tchernikhovsky, *Lyrical Tales and Poems
of Jewish Life*
(translated from the Russian versions of
Vladislav Khodasevich)
Keshet Press

*A Poetic Dialogue with Adam Mickiewicz:
The "Crimean Sonnets"*
(translated from the Polish, with Sonnet Preface,
Sonnet Replies, and Notes)
Bernstein-Verlag Bonn

Enrico Corsi and Francesca Gambino,
Divine Adventure: The Fantastic Travels of Dante
(English verse rendition of the prose translation
by Maria Vera Properzi-Altschuler)
Idea Publications [out of print]

Literary Criticism

*Patterns of Epiphany: From Wordsworth to Tennyson,
Pater, and Barrett Browning*
Southern Illinois University Press

Blake and Goethe: Psychology, Ontology, Imagination
University of Missouri Press

[For e-books on Mickiewicz, Pushkin, and Bjerke
see martinbidney.org]

Made in the USA
Monee, IL
01 July 2023